Builder's Note

When Ben Emory came to visit me in the fall of 1977 to discuss the planning and building of a sailing dinghy, we spent a couple of interesting hours talking design and construction and how best to meet his requirements — a small boat able to take his family, which includes two small children, on picnics to their island in Frenchmans Bay in safety and style. She was to row and sail well, and be able to land on rocky beaches without damaging herself. The rig must stow inside the boat and be simplicity itself.

Ben had with him a copy of the Mystic Seaport monograph on building a copy of the Herreshoff Columbia model dinghies (*Building the Herreshoff Dinghy*, by Barry Thomas, Mystic Seaport, 1977). These boats were considered the ultimate development of the lapstrake yacht tender, without which no yacht owner, or indeed his professional captain, felt his equipment was complete. The Herreshoff Manufacturing Co. built dozens of these fine little craft. They were about 11 1/2 feet long, lightly built with copper-riveted lapstrake planking of thin cedar, and had a small daggerboard and a large leg-of-mutton sail with a long overhanging boom. They were almost invariably varnished inside and out, and were beautiful examples of the art of building small boats.

Lapstrake construction, while producing a strong, light boat, is very vulnerable to plank damage when used as a beach boat on rough, rocky Maine shores. The thin planking is only supported at the edges, and does not bear on the frames across the whole width of the planks. Sooner or later, one of the bottom planks is split by people moving about in the boat while grounded on the beach. When this happens, repair is difficult. So it was decided to go to smooth-planked carvel construction, with plank thickness increased from 3/8" to 1/2". Fastenings would be copper rivets. We also changed to a pivoted centerboard with a longer case so that the centerboard could strike bottom without harm to itself or the trunk. The sprit rig is a favorite of mine, and I was able to convince Ben that the shorter spars, lack of a head-knocking boom, and general simplicity of the rig made it more suitable for his needs than the original leg-of-mutton.

The final concern we had with the design was size. Was the boat large enough for two adults and two children and their gear? If we enlarged it, would it be too heavy to handle on the beach? It was decided that I would expand the boat by 10%, which brought the length up to about 12 1/2 feet. This was easily done by multiplying the offsets, station spacing, waterline interval, etc., by 1.1 before making the molds and setting up the boat. This worked out fine in practice, and caused no problems.

So the end result is a larger version of the Herreshoff dinghy, built to slightly heavier scantlings and a different construction method, with another rig and centerboard configuration. She rows and sails beautifully, thanks to her superior model, and she does all the things Ben wanted. She looks good and was fun to build. Ben is pleased, I'm pleased, and I trust that N.G.H. is still resting comfortably.

—Joel White
Brooklin, ME

How to Build the Catspaw Dinghy

A Boat for Oar & Sail

By the Editors of WoodenBoat Magazine

Photographs by Jon Wilson and William Lamprell
Plans by Spencer Lincoln

WoodenBoat Books

Published by WoodenBoat Publications
Naskeag Road
Brooklin, Maine 04616

Introduction

"Building a Dinghy for Oar and Sail" originally appeared in *WoodenBoat* Magazine (issues 26,27 & 28). We had always wanted to publish a true how-to-build article in *WoodenBoat* since its very beginning. It always seemed simple enough, yet we were never able to organize the finances, the builder, and the photographer at one time, until we saw our chance to take advantage of Joel White's having built the 12 1/2' dinghy for Mr. Ben Emory.

All the requirements were met: We could photograph the process in detail, develop a set of working drawings for Joel's modification, publish them in the article without concern for designers' fees (which prevent a great many people from ever starting out), and help alert readers to the existence of this handsome, yet simple and practical small boat.

We owe a great deal to Barry Thomas, and to Mystic Seaport, for having the good sense to publish the monograph *Building the Herreshoff Dinghy*, for we feel that it is one of the best publications to come from that museum. The departures Joel made from the original design were for specific reasons, to suit specific needs. It made so much sense in so many ways that we could not resist covering the process in detail, especially since it would be the second boat built on the molds, which would mean our saving some lofting and pattern-making steps. For those to whom this boat makes sense, we're very proud to offer this first of what we hope will be a long line of how-to-build articles and monographs on unique and practical wooden boats.

—Jon Wilson

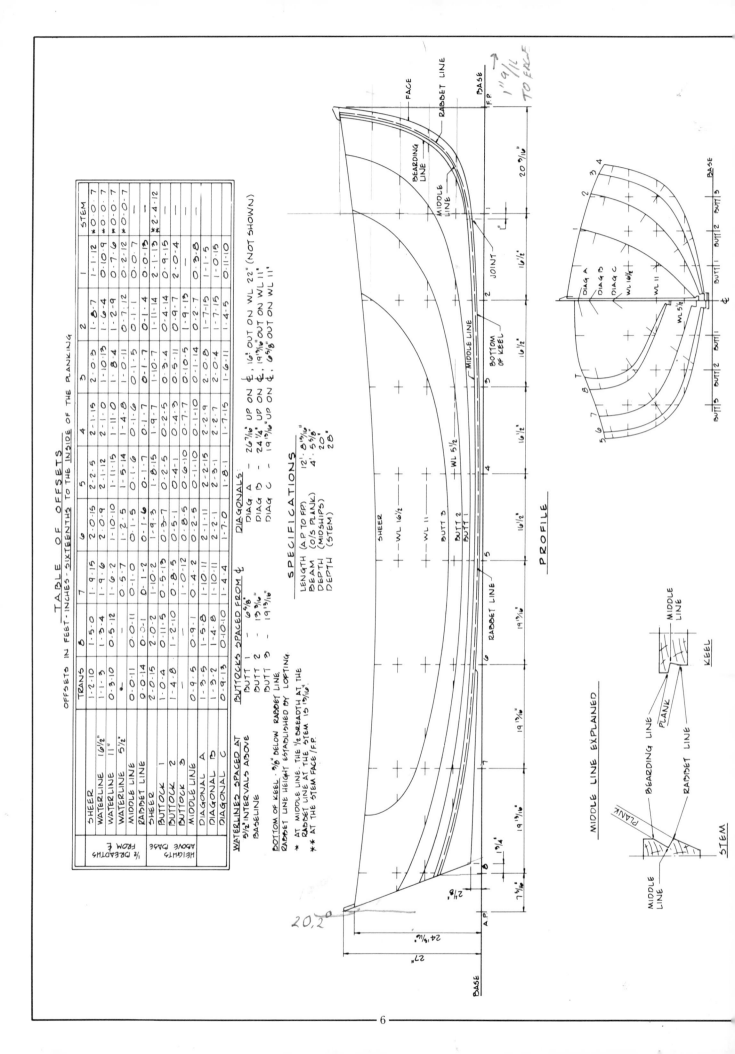

TABLE OF OFFSETS

OFFSETS IN FEET-INCHES-SIXTEENTHS TO THE INSIDE OF THE PLANKING

		TRANS	8	7	6	5	4	3	2	1	STEM
½ BREADTHS FROM ₵	SHEER	1-2-10	1-5-0	1-9-15	2-0-15	2-2-5	2-1-15	2-0-5	1-8-7	1-1-12	0-0-7
	WATERLINE 16½	1-1-3	1-3-4	1-9-6	2-0-9	2-1-0	2-1-0	1-10-13	1-6-4	0-10-9	*0-0-7
	WATERLINE 11	0-3-10	0-5-12	0-6-2	1-10-10	1-11-0	1-11-0	1-8-4	1-2-9	0-7-6	**0-0-7
	WATERLINE 5½	—	—	0-5-7	0-5-7	1-2-5	1-4-8	1-5-14	1-2-12	0-2-12	*0-0-7
	MIDDLE LINE	0-0-11	0-0-11	0-1-0	0-1-5	0-1-6	0-1-7	0-1-5	0-1-1	0-0-7	—
	RABBET LINE	0-0-14	0-0-1	0-1-2	0-1-5	0-1-7	0-1-7	0-1-4	0-1-4	0-0-15	—
HEIGHTS ABOVE BASE	SHEER	2-0-15	2-0-2	1-10-2	1-9-3	1-8-15	1-9-7	1-10-7	1-11-14	2-1-15	**2-4-12
	BUTTOCK 1	1-0-4	0-11-5	0-5-0	0-3-7	0-2-5	0-2-5	0-3-4	0-4-14	0-9-15	—
	BUTTOCK 2	1-4-8	1-2-10	0-8-5	0-5-1	0-4-1	0-4-3	0-5-11	0-9-7	2-0-4	—
	BUTTOCK 3	—	—	0-9-12	0-8-5	0-6-10	0-7-7	0-9-7	1-9-15	0-3-8	—
	MIDDLE LINE	0-9-5	0-9-1	0-4-2	0-2-5	0-2-10	0-2-4	0-2-0	0-2-7	0-3-8	—
	DIAGONAL A	1-3-5	1-5-8	1-10-11	2-1-11	2-2-15	2-2-9	2-0-8	1-7-15	1-1-5	—
	DIAGONAL B	1-3-2	1-4-8	1-10-11	2-3-1	2-3-1	2-2-1	2-0-4	1-7-15	1-0-15	—
	DIAGONAL C	0-9-13	0-10-10	1-4-4	1-7-15	1-8-1	1-7-15	1-6-11	1-4-5	1-6-10	—

WATERLINES SPACED AT 5½" INTERVALS ABOVE BASELINE

BOTTOM OF KEEL, ⅜" BELOW RABBET LINE. RABBET LINE HEIGHT ESTABLISHED BY LOFTING.

* AT MIDDLE LINE, THE ½ BREADTH AT THE RABBET LINE AT THE STEM IS 13/16".
** AT THE STEM FACE/F.P.

BUTTOCKS SPACED FROM ₵
BUTT 1 - 0⅝"
BUTT 2 - 13³/₁₆"
BUTT 3 - 19¹³/₁₆"

DIAGONALS
DIAG A - 26⁷/₁₆" UP ON ₵, 16" OUT ON WL 22" (NOT SHOWN)
DIAG B - 24¼" UP ON ₵, 19¹³/₁₆" OUT ON WL 11"
DIAG C - 19¹³/₁₆" UP ON ₵, 6⅝" OUT ON WL 11"

SPECIFICATIONS

LENGTH (AP TO FP) 12'-8½/₁₆"
BEAM (O/S PLANK) 4'-5⅝"
DEPTH (MIDSHIPS) 20"
DEPTH (STEM) 28"

PROFILE

MIDDLE LINE EXPLAINED

STEM — KEEL — PLANK — BEARDING LINE — RABBET LINE — MIDDLE LINE

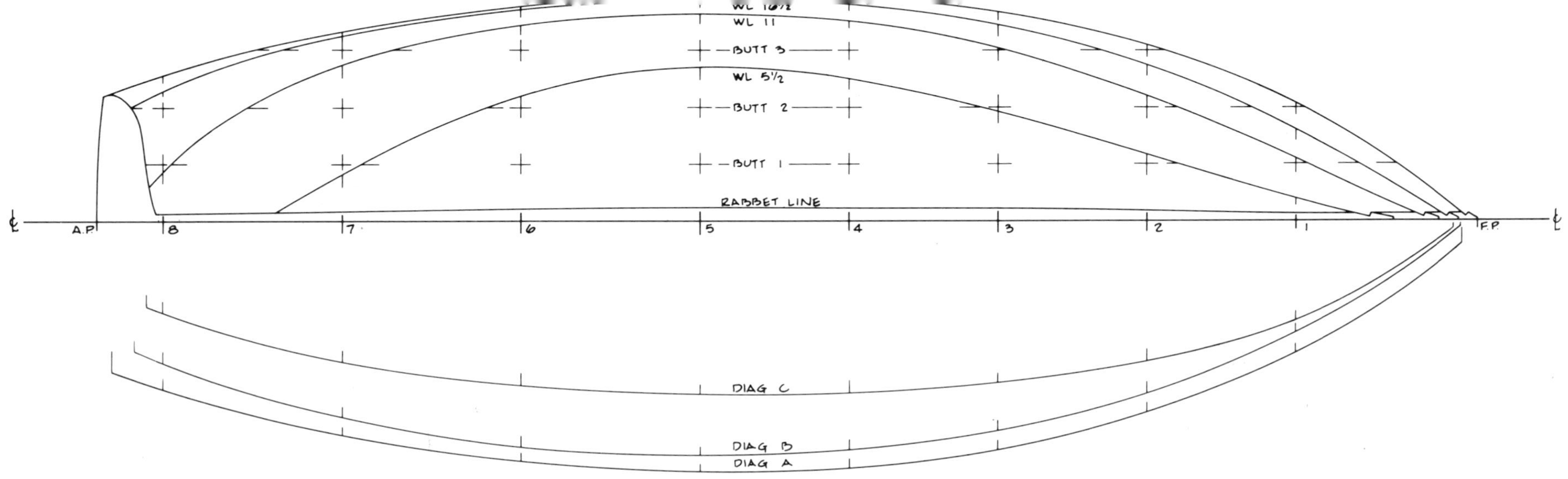
WL 11
BUTT 3
WL 5½
BUTT 2
BUTT 1
RABBET LINE
A.P.
8
7
6
5
4
3
2
1
F.P.
DIAG C
DIAG B
DIAG A

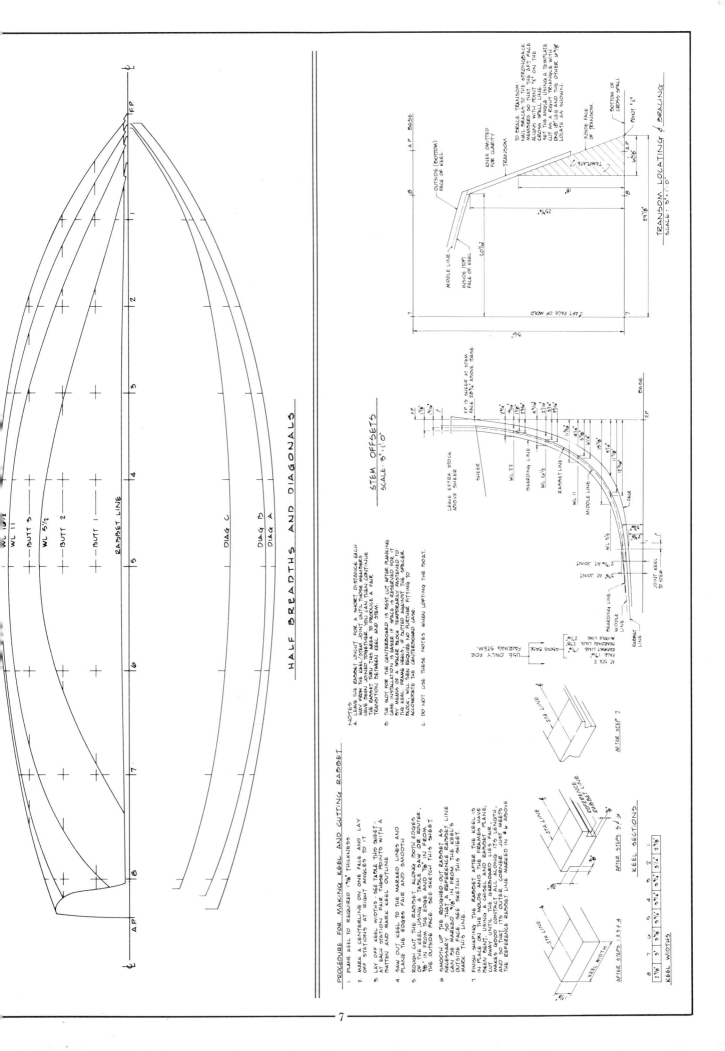

HALF BREADTHS AND DIAGONALS

PROCEDURE FOR MAKING KEEL AND CUTTING RABBET

1. PLANE KEEL TO REQUIRED 1⅞" THICKNESS.
2. MARK A CENTERLINE ON ONE FACE AND LAY OFF STATIONS AT RIGHT ANGLES TO IT.
3. LAY OFF KEEL WIDTHS - SEE TABLE THIS SHEET - AT EACH STATION. FAIR THESE POINTS WITH A BATTEN AND MARK KEEL OUTLINE.
4. SAW OUT KEEL TO THE MARKED LINES AND PLANE THE EDGES FAIR AND SMOOTH.
5. ROUGH CUT THE RABBET ALONG BOTH EDGES OF THE KEEL, USING A TABLE SAW OR ROUTER, ⅜" IN FROM THE EDGE AND ⅞" IN FROM THE OUTSIDE FACE. SEE SKETCH THIS SHEET.
6. SMOOTH UP THE ROUGHED-OUT RABBET AS NECESSARY SO THAT A REFERENCE RABBET LINE CAN BE MARKED ⅜" IN FROM THE KEEL'S OUTSIDE FACE. SEE SKETCH THIS SHEET. MARK THIS LINE.
7. FINISH SHAPING THE RABBET AFTER THE KEEL IS IN PLACE ON THE MOLDS AND THE FRAMES HAVE BEEN BENT. USING A CHISEL AND RABBET PLANE, CUT AWAY UNTIL THE GARBOARD LIES FAIR, MAKES GOOD CONTACT ALL ALONG ITS LENGTH, AND SO THAT ITS OUTER CORNER JUST MEETS THE REFERENCE RABBET LINE MARKED IN #6 ABOVE.

NOTES:

A. LEAVE THE RABBET UNCUT FOR A SHORT DISTANCE EACH WAY FROM THE KEEL/STEM JOINT UNTIL THOSE MEMBERS HAVE BEEN JOINED TOGETHER. YOU CAN THEN CONTINUE THE RABBET THRU THIS AREA TO PRODUCE A FAIR TRANSITION BETWEEN KEEL AND STEM.

B. THE SLOT FOR THE CENTERBOARD IS BEST CUT AFTER PLANKING. CASE INSTALLATION IS EASIER IF SPACE IS RESERVED FOR IT BY MEANS OF A SPACER BLOCK TEMPORARILY FASTENED TO THE KEEL. FRAME HEELS, IF BUTTED AGAINST THE SPACER BLOCK, WILL THEN REQUIRE NO FURTHER FITTING TO ACCOMODATE THE CENTERBOARD CASE.

C. DO NOT USE THESE NOTES WHEN LOFTING THE BOAT.

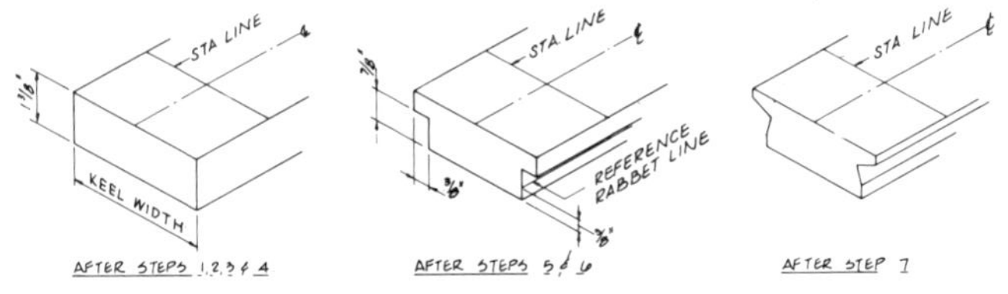
STA LINE
KEEL WIDTH
1⅞"
AFTER STEPS 1,2,3 & 4
REFERENCE RABBET LINE
AFTER STEPS 5 & 6
AFTER STEP 7

KEEL SECTIONS

8	7	6	5	4	3	2	1
2⅞"	3"	3⅝"	3¾"	3¾"	3¾"	3¼"	2⅞"

KEEL WIDTHS

STEM OFFSETS

SCALE: 3" = 1'-0"

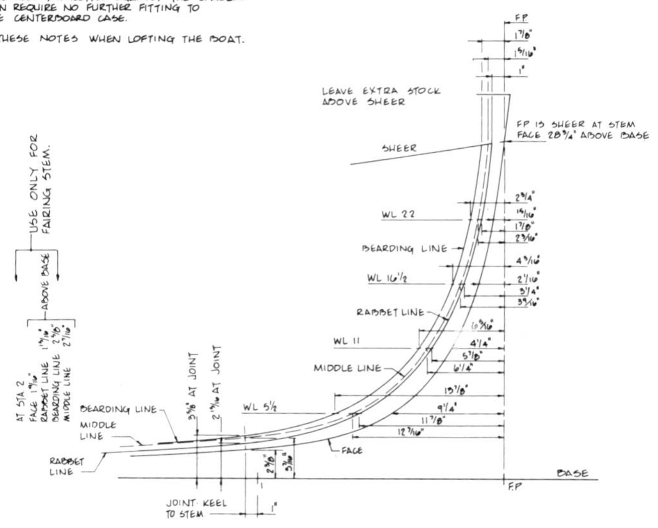
LEAVE EXTRA STOCK ABOVE SHEER
FP IS SHEER AT STEM FACE 28¾" ABOVE BASE
SHEER
WL 22
BEARDING LINE
WL 16½
RABBET LINE
WL 11
MIDDLE LINE
WL 5½
FACE
BASE
FP
JOINT KEEL TO STEM
USE ONLY FOR FAIRING STEM.
ABOVE BASE
AT STA 2
RABBET LINE
BEARDING LINE
MIDDLE LINE

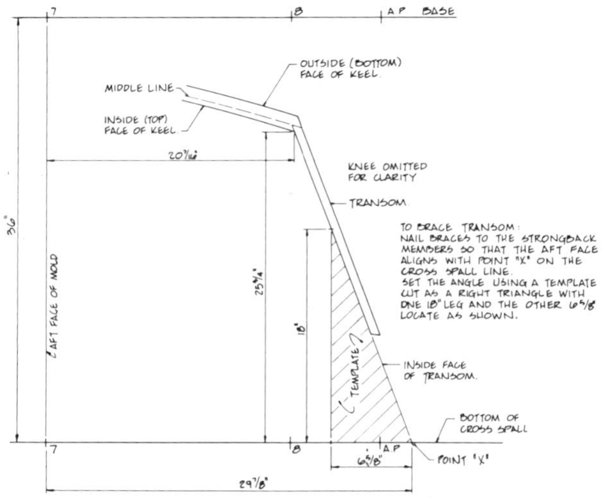
A P BASE
OUTSIDE (BOTTOM) FACE OF KEEL
MIDDLE LINE
INSIDE (TOP) FACE OF KEEL
KNEE OMITTED FOR CLARITY
TRANSOM
TO BRACE TRANSOM:
NAIL BRACES TO THE STRONGBACK MEMBERS SO THAT THE AFT FACE ALIGNS WITH POINT "X" ON THE CROSS SPALL LINE.
SET THE ANGLE USING A TEMPLATE CUT AS A RIGHT TRIANGLE WITH ONE 18" LEG AND THE OTHER 6⅝" LOCATE AS SHOWN.
AFT FACE OF MOLD
TEMPLATE
INSIDE FACE OF TRANSOM.
BOTTOM OF CROSS SPALL
POINT "X"
36"
29⅞"
18"

TRANSOM LOCATING & BRACING

SCALE: 3" = 1'-0"

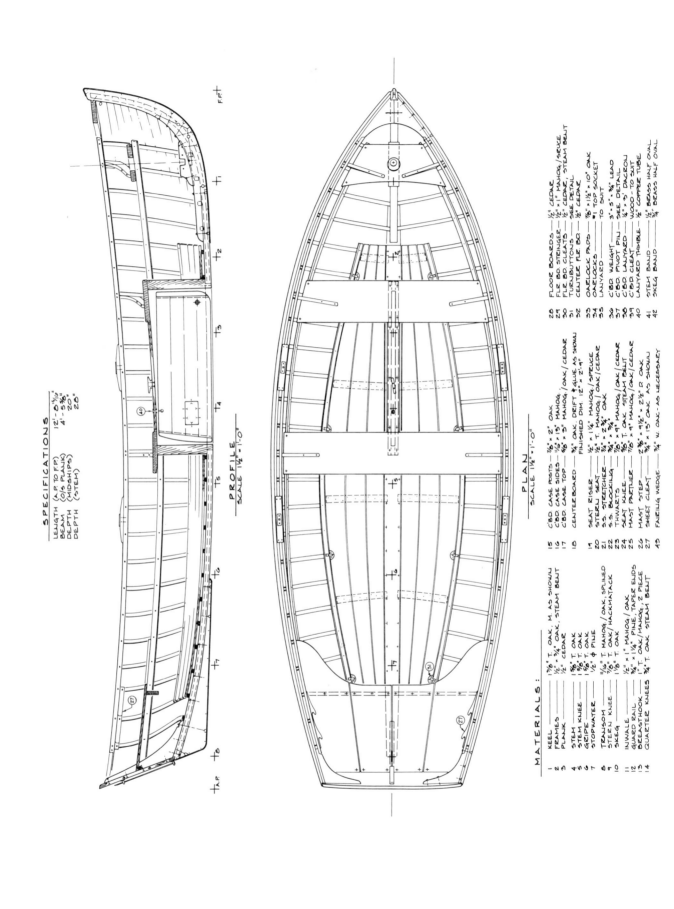

SPECIFICATIONS

LENGTH (A.P. TO F.P.)	12'-0 9/16"
BEAM (O/S PLANK)	4'-5 5/8"
DEPTH (MIDSHIPS)	1'-20"
DEPTH (STEM)	28"

PROFILE
SCALE 1½" = 1'-0"

PLAN
SCALE 1½" = 1'-0"

MATERIALS:

1 KEEL — 1 5/8" T. OAK, M. AS SHOWN
2 FRAMES — ½" × ¾" OAK, STEAM BENT
3 PLANK — ½" CEDAR
4 STEM — 1 5/8" T. OAK
5 GRIPE — 1 5/8" T. OAK
6 STOPWATER — ½" Ø PINE
8 TRANSOM — 11/16" T. MAHOG/OAK, SPLINED
9 STERN KNEE — 7/8" T. OAK/HACKMATACK
10 SKEG — 1 5/8" T. OAK
11 INWALE — ½" × 1" MAHOG/OAK
12 GUARD RAIL — ¾" × 1¼" PINE, TAPER ENDS
13 BREASTHOOK — 1" T. OAK/MAHOG, 2 PIECE
14 QUARTER KNEES — ¾" T. OAK, STEAM BENT

15 C'BD CASE POSTS — ¾" × 2" OAK
16 C'BD CASE SIDES — ½" MAHOG/OAK/CEDAR
17 C'BD CASE TOP — 5/8" × 3" MAHOG/OAK/CEDAR
18 CENTERBOARD — ¾" OAK, DRIFT ↓ GLUE AS SHOWN
     FINISHED DIM. 12" × 2'-4"
19 SEAT RISER — ½" × 1¼" MAHOG/SPRUCE
20 STERN SEAT — ½" T. MAHOG/OAK/CEDAR
21 S.S. STRETCHER — ½" × 2¾" OAK
22 S.S. BLOCKING — ½" × ¾"
23 THWARTS — 7/8" × 9" MAHOG/OAK/CEDAR
24 SEAT KNEE — 5/8" T. OAK, STEAM BENT
25 MAST PARTNER — 7/8" × 4" MAHOG/OAK/CEDAR
26 MAST STEP — 2 3/4" × 9½" × 2½" D OAK
27 SHEET CLEAT — 1½" × 15" OAK AS SHOWN
43 FAIRING WEDGE — ¾" W. OAK, AS NECESSARY

28 FLOOR BOARDS — ¼" CEDAR
29 FLR. BD. STRINGER — ½" × 1" MAHOG/SPRUCE
30 FLR. BD. CLEATS — SEE DETAIL
31 TURNBUTTONS — ½" OAK, STEAM BENT
32 CENTER FLR. BD. — ½" CEDAR
33 OARLOCK PADS — 7/8" × 1½" × 10" OAK
34 OARLOCKS — #1 TOP SOCKET
35 LANYARD — TO SUIT
36 C'BD WEIGHT — 3" × 5" × ¾" LEAD
37 C'BD PIVOT PIN — SEE DETAIL
38 C'BD LANYARD — ¼" × 5' DACRON
39 C'BD CLEAT — WOOD — TO SUIT
40 LANYARD THIMBLE — ½" COPPER TUBE
41 STEM BAND — ½" BRASS HALF OVAL
42 SKEG BAND — ¾" BRASS HALF OVAL

— 8 —

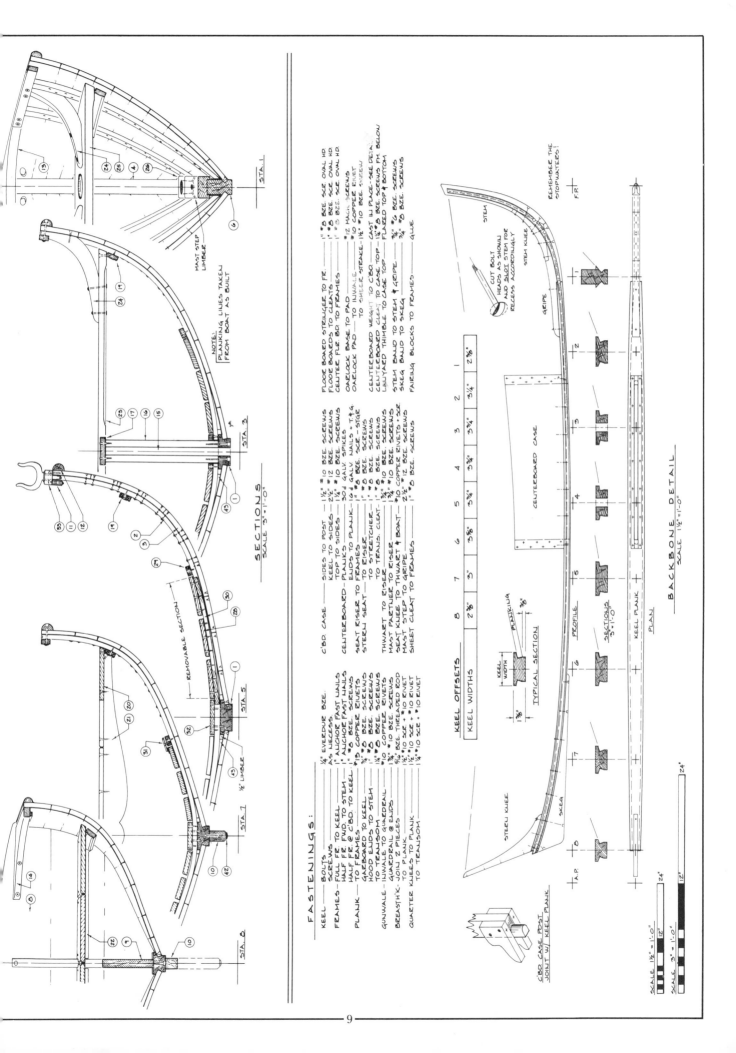

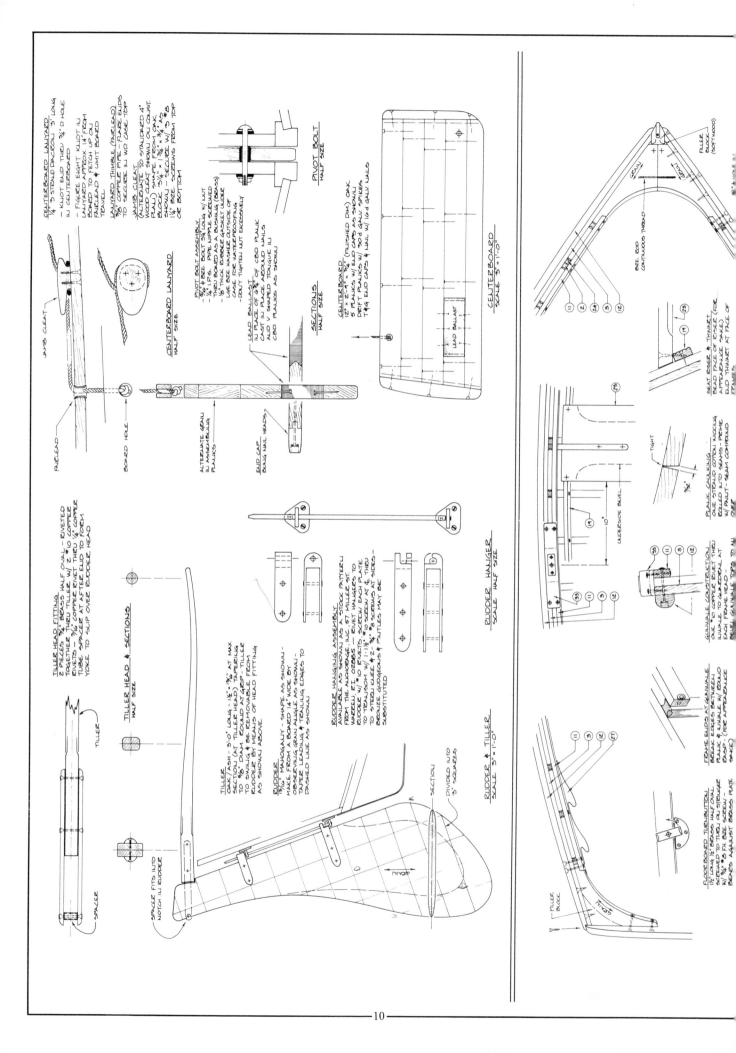

CENTERBOARD LANYARD
¼" Ø STRAND DACRON 5' LONG
- KNOT END THRU ¾" Ø HOLE IN CENTERBOARD

FIGURE EIGHT KNOT IN LANYARD LED APPROX 14 FROM FAIRLEAD TO FETCH UP AT FAIRLEAD & LIMIT BOARD TRAVEL

JAMB CLEAT
(ALTERNATE TO STANDARD 4" WOOD CLEAT SHOWN) OR CUST. MADE - SHAPE FROM OAK BLOCK 2½" × ¾" × 4" AS SHOWN - SECURE W/ 3 #8 1¼" BZE. SCREWS FROM TOP OR BOTTOM

LANYARD THIMBLE (FAIRLEAD)
⅝" Ø COPPER PIPE - FLARE ENDS TO SECURE IN W.O. CASE TOP

JAMB CLEAT

CENTERBOARD LANYARD
HALF SIZE

CENTERBOARD LANYARD

FAIRLEAD

BORED HOLE

ALTERNATE GRAIN IN ASSEMBLING PLANKS

END CAP
BUNG NAIL HEADS

PIVOT BOLT ASSEMBLY
- ¾" Ø BZE. BOLT 3¼" LONG W/ NUT
- 1¼" I.P.S. PIPE NIPPLE SCREWED THRU BOXED AS A BUSHING (BRASS)
- ⅛" THICK RUBBER GASKET OUTSIDE OF CASE FOR WATERPROOFING
- USE BZE. WASHER UNDER CASE FOR WATERPROOFING
- DON'T TIGHTEN NUT EXCESSIVELY

LEAD BALLAST
IN PLACE OF G#% OF CBD PLANK CAST IN PLACE AROUND NAILS AND V SHAPED TONGUE IN CBD PLANKS AS SHOWN

PIVOT BOLT
HALF SIZE

SECTIONS
HALF SIZE

CENTERBOARD
12" × 2'-4" × ¾" (FINISHED DIM.) OAK
5 PLANKS W/ END CAPS AS SHOWN
DRIFT PLANKS W/ 20d GALV SPIKES
T#4 END CAPS & NAIL IN 16d GALV NAILS

LEAD BALLAST

CENTERBOARD
SCALE 3" = 1'-0"

TILLER HEAD FITTING
2 PIECES ¾" BRASS HALF OVAL - RIVETED TOGETHER THRU TILLER W/ 2 #10 COPPER RIVETS - ⅜" COPPER RIVET THRU ¼" COPPER TUBE SPACER AT AFTER END TO FORM YOKE TO SLIP OVER RUDDER HEAD

TILLER HEAD & SECTIONS
HALF SIZE

TILLER

TILLER HEAD

TILLER
OAK/ASH - 5'-0" LONG - 1½" × 1¾" AT MAX SECTION (AT TILLER HEAD) TAPERING TO ⅞" DIAM. ROUND AT GRIP - TILLER TO SWING & BE REMOVABLE FROM RUDDER BY MEANS OF HEAD FITTING AS SHOWN ABOVE

RUDDER
1¾" MAHOGANY - SHAPE AS SHOWN - MAKE FROM A BOARD 14" WIDE BY OBSERVING GRAIN ANGLE AS SHOWN - TAPER LEADING & TRAILING EDGES TO DASHED LINE AS SHOWN

SPACER FITS INTO NOTCH IN RUDDER

SPACER

SECTION

DIVIDED INTO 3" SQUARES

GRAIN

RUDDER & TILLER
SCALE 3" = 1'-0"

RUDDER HANGING ASSEMBLY
AVAILABLE AS SHOWN AS A STOCK PATTERN FROM THE ANCHORAGE, INC., 67 MILLER ST., WAREEM, R.I. 02885 - RIVET HANGERS TO RUDDER W/ #10 RIVETS, SCREW EACH PLATE TO TRANSOM W/ 1-1½" #10 SCREW AT ¢ & THRU TO STERN KNEE & 2-¾" #8 SCREWS AT SIDES - BRONZE GUDGEONS & PINTLES MAY BE SUBSTITUTED

RUDDER HANGER
SCALE HALF SIZE

SEAT EDGER & THWART
HEAD FACE OF EDGER (FOR APPEARANCE OF THWART) SCREW TO END THWART AT FACE OF FRAMES

FILLER BLOCK

GRAIN

BZE E20
CONTINUOUS THREAD

① ⑤ ②④ ⑤ ⑫

② ⑭

UNDERSIDE BEVEL

10"

TIGHT

⑤ ⑪ ⑤ ⑫

PLANK CAULKING
ONE STRAND COTTON CAULKING ROLLED INTO SEAMS PRIME W/ PAINT - SEAM COMPOUND OVER

GUNWALE CONSTRUCTION
GLUE #10 COPPER RIVET THRU IN WALE TO GUNDERHOLD AT EACH FRAME HEAD - BEVEL GUNWALE TOPS TO AN

FRAME END AT GUNWALE
BREAK EDGES BETWEEN PLANK & INWALE W/ ROUND RASP - (FOR APPEARANCE SAKE)

FLOOR BOARD TURNBUTTON
1½" LONG ½" BRASS HALF OVAL SCREWED TO TURN ON STRINGER W/ ⅝" #8 F.H. BZE SCREW - BORES AGAINST BRASS PLATE

FILLER BLOCK

GRAIN

① ⑤ ⑫ ②⑦

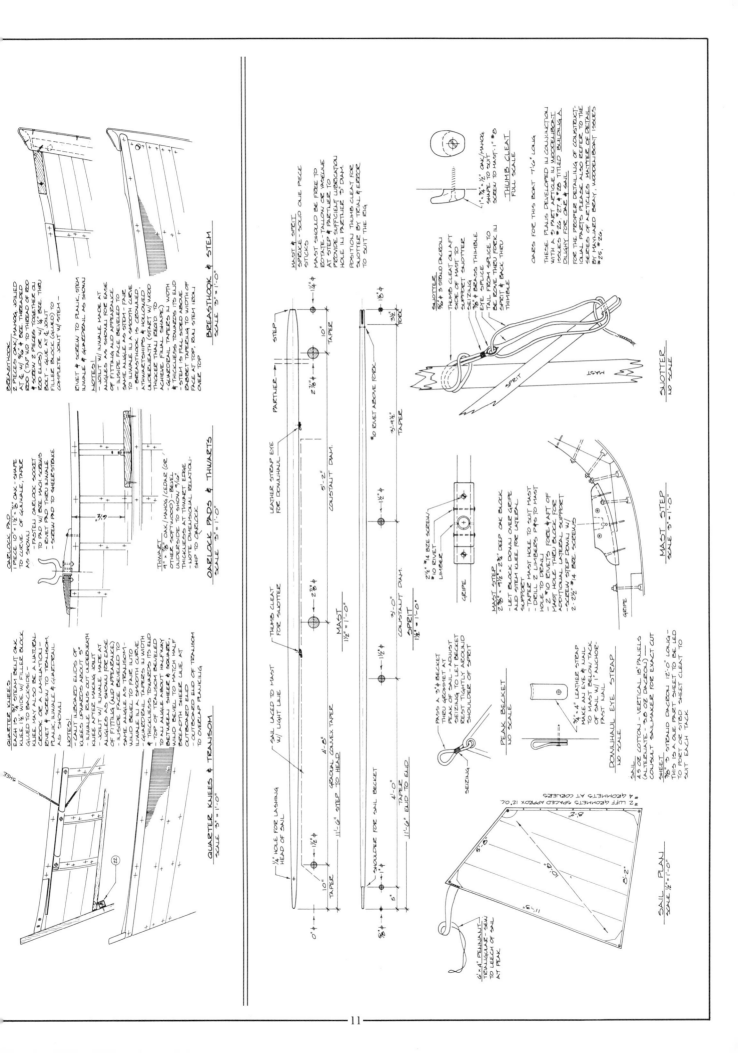

1 Because this is the second boat that Joel White has built to this
design, it was not necessary to construct new molds. (*For those in-
terested in mold-making and other preliminaries,* WoodenBoat *Nos.
11 and 12 have articles on lofting, and there is an article in No. 13 on
making molds.*) Here construction of the building jig has begun with
two strongbacks blocked to a convenient working height. Joel White
found the full lofting to be unnecessary. By using the offsets directly to
make each mold, everything faired out well in three dimensions. (Of
course, since the offsets are given to the inside of the planking, it was
necessary to deduct the thickness of the frames when marking the outline of each mold.) Joel did lay down enough of the stem and forebody
to pick up the rabbet and bearding lines, however, and the results of
this minor lofting are shown on the lines plan.

2 The parallel strongback timbers are leveled
athwartships and fore and aft, then nailed to the
blocking.

6 (above) This is the stem assembly just
before it was bolted together. It consists
of the gripe, stem knee, and the stem piece
itself. We will refer to this three-piece
assembly as the "stem" from here on. Herreshoff's shop used two steam-bent laminations,
running full length for a stem, but Joel
White's custom is to use fabricated stems like
that shown here.

5 Here the molds are all set up, squared to the centerline, plumbed, and braced
to each other.

3 (below) Each mold has a cross spall to support it at a convenient working height. For this boat the cross spalls are all on an arbitrary baseline, parallel to the waterlines and a little higher than the sheer. Small wood blocks are nailed to the strongbacks at each station to aid in locating and fastening the molds.

4 (right) The 'midship mold is strongly braced, lending support to the other molds, which are plumbed and held in that position with temporary battens tied to the 'midship mold. Herreshoff's shop used a mold at every other frame, eliminating the need for ribbands, but in this case, since there was no thought of mass production, the molds were placed on the seven station lines. (*See* Building the Herreshoff Dinghy *for more discussion of these setup methods.*)

7 (left below) The stem is clamped to the table, and the rabbet is cut. The rabbet is defined by the rabbet line and bearding line, obtained from the lofting, and its depth and angle are cut to fit a small piece of 1/2"-thick cedar, representing the planking which, later on, must lie in it.

8 (above) The rabbet is deliberately stopped a few inches short of the forward end of the keel, to be finished when the keel is bolted in place. This enables a smooth transition between the stem and keel rabbets. The heads of the carriage bolts used to assemble the stem are ground flat on opposite sides, so as to fit within the face width of the finished stem. Once the rabbet is cut, the sides of the stem between the rabbet line and stem face are beveled off flat.

9 (right) The keel, which swells at mid-length to accommodate the centerboard trunk, is marked off with a batten.

10 The keel is sawn to shape.

11 (below) The stem has been beveled off, the keel has been rough-rabbetted on the table saw, and the two have been bolted together. The aft end of the keel tucks up quickly and had to be steamed. It is shown here being removed from the steambox, after which it will be turned end for end and clamped into the notches in the molds. At the Herreshoff yard, where several dinghies were built at once, the keel was steamed and bent over a separate form, then dropped into place when needed.

12 (right) The keel is held in place with C-clamps and a strut from overhead. Note the roughed-out rabbet.

one

Building

two

three

four

one — Three mahogany planks are cut and checked against their pattern for size. Because the transom is to be varnished, the planks are taken from a single piece of mahogany.

two — The plank edges are squared up and straightened with the table saw.

three — The final truing up is done by hand. The planks are placed together and checked with a straightedge to be sure they form a flat plane.

four — Because the planks are to be splined together, a groove is cut in both edges of both seams.

13 (left below) While the keel is held to the approximate bend by another strut from the overhead, the skeg, which goes in the way of the quick bend aft, is clamped to the keel over a small spacer block in order to over-bend the keel slightly. This prevents the keel from straightening too much when the skeg is later removed for drilling, bedding, and fastening.

14 (below) The transom is set in place, braced, and attached to the keel by the stern knee. Note the supports from the strongback to the transom, holding it at the proper height and rake. Also visible is the taut string centerline used to position the molds, the stem, and the transom.

he Transom

seven

eight

five — After the splines are cut and fitted individually, the planks are pushed together, without glue, for an assembled fit.

six — The assembly is checked with a straightedge and "kissed" with a plane as needed. The transom is then clamped together and checked with straightedges for flatness under pressure.

seven — The plank edges and splines are spread with glue and the transom is assembled.

eight — The transom is clamped together with the straightedges to assure flatness. Wax paper prevents the straightedges and clamps from sticking to the transom when the glue cures.

15 The ribbands are set in notches and fastened in place to provide a temporary form over which the frames can be bent. The lines and offsets are to the inside of the planking, and when making the molds it was necessary to deduct the thickness of the frames. The molds were notched so the ribbands would lie flush when the first boat was built, so the notches were already there when this boat was started.

16 (left) This is how the ribbands attached to the stem and tran so their outside surfaces correspond the inside faces of the frames. The stopwaters at the joints of the stem knee were driven after the rabbet w marked — but before it was cut since boring for them is easier that way.

17 (below) The oak frames are steamed after being brushed with a mixture of linseed oil and tur pentine to help preserve them. A p pane burner heats a water tank, whi is placed inside a welded enclosure t retain the heat. A rubber hose carri the steam to the steambox.

21 Nails prevent the frames from springing away from the ribbands, but they must be removed as the planking progresses or the boat can't be lifted off the building jig.

22 (above) At first only every other frame is bent in. These alternate frames are allowed to cool, and the remaining frames are then bent in between them. This prevents the ribbands from flattening out between the molds under pressure from too many freshly bent frames.

23 (right) Except right amidships, the frames are allowed to sweep naturally toward the ends of the boat, from an even spacing at the keel. At the rail, their heads are kept more or less evenly spaced as well — partly by measurement and partly by eye. Plans are almost always drawn to show steam-bent frames running exactly perpendicular to the centerline, but in practice, unless the frames are bent over the molds the way Herreshoff's builders did it, they usually fan out near the bow and stern as they lie naturally against the ribbands.

8 & 19 The first frame to be bent is located just aft of ~~the~~ centerboard trunk and runs from rail ~~to r~~ail. Rushed from the steambox, it is ~~qui~~ckly clamped to the keel, with a soft-~~woo~~d block between the frame and the ~~cla~~mp to prevent damage and to force it to ~~lie~~ tightly across the full width of the keel. ~~A t~~emporary spacer block representing the ~~wid~~th and position of the centerboard ~~tru~~nk can be seen just forward of this ~~fra~~me. Frames in the way of the trunk will ~~fit~~ tightly against this block, assuring a ~~goo~~d fit once the trunk is installed. The ~~fra~~me is held in contact with the ribbands, ~~and~~ bent around the hull, where it is tem-~~por~~arily nailed in place with 4d finish

nails. The frames weren't continuous in Herreshoff dinghies, but were joined together on top of the keel with floor timbers, a practice that perhaps carried over from that yard's larger boats.

20 The same process is repeated on every other frame, working fore and aft from amidships.

24 At the bow, the frames are not continuous rail to rail, but are in halves, stepping against and fastened to the stem. Here, a landing is smoothed up for the heel of one of the half-frames.

25 The heel of a half-frame is drilled for a fastening.

26 The bevels for the heels of the half-frames in the bow are lifted off and cut prior to steaming and these frames are fastened with bronze Anchorfast nails. The heels of the half-frames in way of the centerboard trunk are screwed to the keel while each of the continuous frames is nailed to the keel with two Anchorfast nails.

27 The last of the frames is shown installed in the way of the centerboard trunk. The boat is ready for planking.

28 A landing is prepared for the garboard plank by finishing off the rough rabbet in the keel and by gluing oak wedges in place on all the frames (except the half-frames up forward). But first, the garboard's top edge is lined off with a batten and marked on each frame. By using a small straightedge between this line and the middle line of the keel rabbet, the flange of the rabbet (that part between the middle line and the bearding line) can be dressed down and the shape of each wedge can be templated. Wedges are made up from scrap frame stock and are glued in place with contact cement. A space is left between them and the edge of the keel as a limber.

29 & 30 So they'll bend more easily, the forward ends of the garboards a the next two or three planks are steamed. The starboard garboa being clamped in place here, be ning with the forward end. The garboard is already done. Whe

32 It's easier to work with steamed planks than cold planks that fight back. A dry cedar plank that has lost much of its natural flexibility yet must twist or bend greatly to conform to the shape of the boat should always be put into the steambox for a few minutes to be softened up before it is hung.

33 The insides of the planks at the turn of the bilge, starting with No. 4, have to be hollowed or backed out so they fit tightly agai the frames all across their width. One eighth inch or so of extra thick ness must be given to these bilge strakes so the finished hull will be of uniform thickness (a good point to remember when having the plank ing stock milled out).

hey have cooled overnight, they'll by unclamped and trimmed as needed for a good ght fit against the keel and stem rabbets. The rough shape is obtained by spiling, nd an index mark is placed on both the stem and the spiling batten as an aid in loca- ng the plank itself when it is time to clamp it in place. When the plank is pulled om the steambox, it cools off quickly, so it's a good idea to have the clamps and ads at hand as well as to make the marks as noted above. Two pairs of hands make e job easier. One person gets the hood (forward) end in position and clamped hile the other supports the weight of the plank's after end. Steaming the garboards and clamping them on late in the day is a good idea, as they can have all night to cool off without holding up any work. Next morning they can be taken off one at a time and carefully fitted to the rabbet before being permanently fastened in place.

31 Planks are fastened to the frames with copper rivets, while screws are used in way of the oak backbone. The after end of each plank is screwed to the transom as well. A sliding bar clamp is used here to draw this newly hung plank up tightly against its neighbor—an effective technique for the first few planks until the span and hull curvature become too great.

34 Planks are wedged against each other for fastening as shown when the sliding bar clamp is no longer usable. A small screw whose point projects through the wedging pad and bites into the frame keeps the pad from slip- ping when the wedge is driven. Here, the screw's head is hidden under the C-clamp. The ½" planking used on this boat is about the thinnest practical for carvel construction, as it still assures a good caulking job with seams that won't leak later on. Care must be taken to get good fits along each plank's edge and to draw planks closely together before fastening.

35 In a small boat like this with an unmitered transom, planks can be run out beyond the transom and then cut off flush, as is being done here, after they have been fitted and fastened.

36 Frame heads are being sawn off to release the boat from the building form so it can be lifted off and turned over. Care must be taken while driving the plank fastenings that those in the way of ribbands are not driven all the way through the ribbands, which would, in effect, nail the boat to its building form.

Planking

Deciding how many planks there will be to go from the keel to the rail and where their seams will fall is called lining off, and the process depends a great deal on one's eye, along with good judgment. The boat's seams are puttied flush, and for that reason perhaps lining off is less critical than in a lapstrake boat, where each individual plank shows clearly. Even so, you should try to get the planks to taper evenly as they approach the bow and stern, and to have their hood ends at the stem more or less even in width. There are many ways to achieve this, but the method described here is what Joel White used on this boat and it seems to be as simple and effective as any.

Joel lays out his plank widths on the amidship frame where the girth is greatest. Using 10 planks per side, he makes the garboard widest, the bilge planks narrowest, and to the width of the sheer strake so it will appear as wide below the guard raid as the others. Plank widths vary from 3-4¼", and their widths are noted on the construction plans.

1 To find the plank widths graphically (between the broad and sheer strakes) at any station, draw an upright line where the vertical distance between A-A and B-B equals the station girth. Then measure the individual plank widths along it. When laying out this diagram, vertical distances are full scale but since no measurements are taken along the horizontal, its length (scale) is optional.

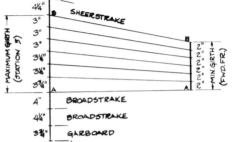

2 With the plank lines established, it is time to make up and hang the garboard planks after first determining their shape by spiling. Each builder has his own method, and this is Joel White's. Like most all other methods, this one begins by tacking on a spiling batten. One-quarter inch or 5/16 inch scrap pine or cedar will do nicely as long as it has width enough to take the same lay as the finished plank, yet lie within that plank's boundaries as marked on the frames. The perpendicular distance between the edge of the batten and the keel rabbet is measured every 8 to 10 inches and marked on the spiling batten. Plank widths are noted on the batten as well.

3 After an indexing mark is made on both the batten and the keel or stem to show their longitudinal relationship (a step needed only for the garboard), the batten can be taken off the boat and temporarily nailed to a suitable piece of planking stock. Here, the procedure is simply reversed; that is, each indicated measurement is laid off and marked out square from the spiling batten onto the planking stock to indicate the lower edge of the garboard where it will fit against the keel. The numbers indicating the plank widths are transferred along with the above-mentioned index line, after which there is no further use for the spiling batten. It can be set aside for use on the next plank.

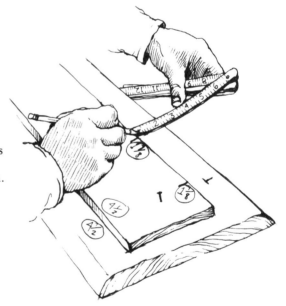

4 The marks indicating the lower edge of the garboard plank must now be connected and faired. To do this a 14-foot long fairing or lining batten is used, which is about 3/8" by 3/4" in section. Nails can be driven at about every other mark and the batten adjusted until it is eye sweet and still hits most of the marks. The plank edge can now be drawn in pencil and, setting off the width measurements from this line, marks showing the plank's upper edge are made. The fairing batten can now be removed and used on the plank's other edge in the very same way.

The top edges of the garboard and broad strakes are lined out by eye and marked on each frame. Keep the lining battens on the marks already made on the 'midship mold and be sure to bring the end of the garboard up on the stem (toward the sheer) as far as practical; it makes the rest of the planks better shaped. The space from the top edge of the broad strake to the sheer can now be lined off more mechanically, and plank widths can be determined at any point along their length by use of the planking lay-out diagram shown in figure 1. This device is much like the one described by Barry Thomas and used at Herreshoff's shop, except it is made up so the plank widths between the broad and the sheer strakes at the forward end of the boat are all equal, rather than holding to a proportionally smaller version of the plank widths amidships. You will note that the plank lines are indicated on the construction plan—a feature that may make lining off easier than starting from scratch.

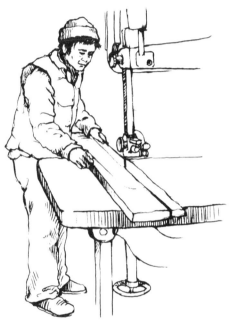

5 After sawing slightly outside the lines, this plank will be mated; that is, used as a pattern for its counterpart on the other side of the boat.

6 The first plank is shown here temporarily nailed to another piece of stock from which its mate is being sawn out. The two planks stay nailed together and are treated as one until their edges have been planed down the line.

7 The two planks, still temporarily nailed together, are planed on each edge down to the marked line. Another less common way of getting out planks for a small boat is to use stock that is thick enough to be resawn into two individual planks after shaping. The cedar boat boards used here, however, weren't that thick and planks had to be made individually. Caulking bevels are now planed on the individual planks mostly by eye with an occasional check of the plank against its landing, which in this case is the keel. Caulking bevels go on only the lower edge of the planks, that is, the edge closest to the keel; the other edge is left square. Plank seams should all be tight on the inside and open no more than 1/16 inch on the outside of the boat. Depth of the caulking seam bevel is about 2/3 of the plank thickness, or in this case about 5/16 to 3/8 inch.

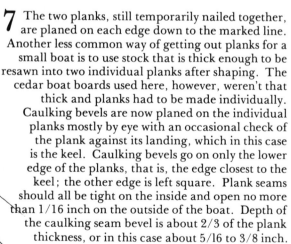

8 Planking proceeds in about the same way for the remaining strakes, except those at the turn of the bilge must be hollowed or backed out before they are hung. An extra 1/8 inch should have been allowed on them during their original milling, otherwise they'll be too thin when the boat is smoothed up. The extent of hollowing can be easily determined by using a templating tool, available in any hardware store. A wooden plane with a slight crown to its sole is usually used to back out planks, although an iron plane whose blade has been ground convex can be used in a pinch. Joel White and some other professionals use an electric plane with convex knives, but this tool is not found in most home workshops.

37 The two cross spalls nailed temporarily in place here were cut to length before the boat was lifted off her form, thus assuring no change in the boat's beam. Once rightside up, the rivets must be set with their heads far enough below the surface of the planking so they'll not be hit when the hull is planed smooth. Two persons are needed for setting nails; one holds the backing dolly against the frame while the other sets the nail from the outside using a hammer and nail set.

38 (below) Burrs are then slipped over the ends of the nails, a frame at a time, and the nails are clipped back to the right length for riveting (about the diameter of a nail beyond the face of the burr). Nails are clipped with dulled cutters. The extra squeeze needed to use the cutters flares out the nail at that point so the burr will not shake loose while others are being riveted.

39 (right) Riveting is mostly a one-person task, with one arm inside the boat and one outside. The area in the boat's bottom that can't be reached this way must be riveted with the help of another person.

43 The slot is cut through the keel to match the assembled trunk and is started by boring a 7/8" hole at each end. (The heels or tenons of the posts have been shaped to fit against the ends of the slot, which are semicircular rather than square—a great timesaver). These holes in the keel are then connected, using a sabre saw. The trunk assembly is given a dry fitting and, after being shaved down here and there for good wood-to-wood contact, is held in position while screw holes are bored through the keel and into it. The trunk is then taken out while a bead of sealant is squeezed out on top of the keel.

44 Having previously been assured of a good fit, the trunk is placed into position with confidence for the final time.

45 With the boat turned upside down and a chisel holding up the end of the trunk, screws are driven to fasten the trunk in place.

40 (below) Tools for riveting are shown here and consist of a nail set, a pair of blunted cutters, a small ball-peen hammer, and a backing dolly. This dolly, which is made from a piece of bronze shafting, has a hole in one end for use in setting the nails and a raised bushing on the other end, which is placed against the nail's head during the riveting operation.

41 & 42 Sides of the centerboard trunk are of 11/16" mahogany; posts are from 7/8 x 2" oak and allow for a 3/4"-thick board. Before being screwed together, a strand of cotton wicking is laid along each side of each post and marine sealer (3M No. 5200 or equivalent) is spread there as well. Lower edges of the trunk sides are rough cut to a pattern before a final fit is made against the keel. The pattern is quickly made by tracing the shape of the *outside* of the keel in way of the trunk onto a piece of pattern stock and then sawing it out. The posts are notched back an inch or so for a landing on top of the keel.

6 Looking down at the stern knee. Note how the frame cants aft.

47 The outside of the hull, before caulking, is smoothed up fair using planes and sandpaper. On a small boat like this, which can be turned and moved to a comfortable working position and which is planked with soft cedar, smoothing up isn't too big a job. Care must be taken, however, to avoid slivering the wood, which, because of its rather wild grain, has this tendency. Plane with care and keep the iron sharp! Numbers 60 and 100 sandpaper wrapped around a cork block and used diagonally across the planking takes over after planing, helped out by some elbow grease.

48 Marking for the painted waterline was done with the boat upside down and leveled athwartships. A string, stretched between a leveled straightedge at the stern and another at the bow, is moved in until it touches the hull amidships at which point the freeboard (the distance between the string and the sheer) is noted. The freeboard is checked in the same way on the other side and the hull is adjusted, if need be, until both the port and starboard freeboard are equal. Now the process of spotting in the waterline can commence.

It goes this way: You mark the waterline's position amidships with a small sharp-pointed tack, placed just above the string. More tacks, spaced about 8" apart, will be stuck in forward and aft of this one continuing on to the ends of the boat. To establish the location of each tack, you keep moving the string inward along its straightedge until it is almost in contact with the hull at the place you want to mark. Care must be taken that the string doesn't ride up on the hull (which it tends to do even though it is generally held in place by the tacks), and that the tacks are put in so their points are on a level with the string.

49 Near the stern, where the skeg interferes, a spirit level is used to bridge the distance between the string and the hull. And again at the bow, because the waterline there is somewhat hollow, a spirit level is used.

52 With the hull prime-painted and its seams and fastening heads puttied with marine seam compound, she is ready for seats, floorboards, rails, and other finishing touches.

53 A pattern is made for the underside of the mast step so it will fit nicely upon the gripe, and the desired location for its fastenings are indicated on the pattern so they miss the bolts.

50 For easy painting, the waterline is scribed into the hull, or incised with a fine-toothed saw or a bent-over file whose tang has been sharpened. A fair curve is first formed with a light batten nailed along the line of the tacks and this batten is then used to guide the scribing tool.

51 Caulking a little boat like this is easiest done with cotton wicking and a roller. (If you don't have such a tool, you can make one out of a big washer and a wooden handle. Grind the washer's edge so it's fairly sharp.) A single strand of wicking is laid out along each seam, after which it takes only a few minutes to roll it firmly into place. For caulking, the seams should be tight in the inside. Even if they were that way when the planks were hung, you may find that some shrinkage has occurred in the meantime and that light shows through them. If this has happened, it is a simple matter to unleash some steam underneath the boat for an hour or two and swell the seams tight again. In any event, you'll want to give the boat a coat of primer inside and out right after she is caulked, to stablize the planking, firm up the caulking, and help keep her from opening up her seams again and spitting out their caulking.

A caulking iron and mallet are used wherever the roller won't fit — like along the garboard seams. Take it easy when caulking around the transom or you'll force the planking away from it; a putty knife may be best there.

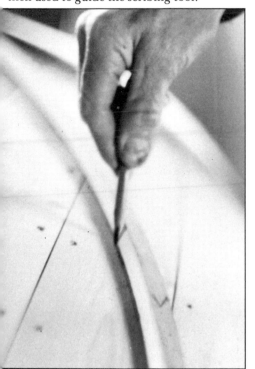

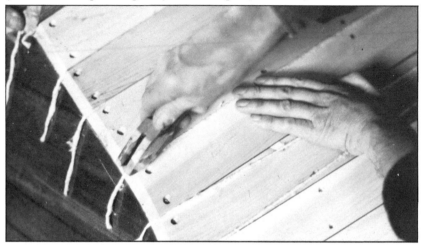

54 It's important that the step be let down over the gripe so it can resist the sideways thrust of the mast while sailing. A couple of big bronze screws hold it in place, and limber holes are bored uphill into the mast socket so water won't collect here. It's a whole lot easier to install the mast step at this stage when there is good access, and besides it can be used as a target for the hole in the partners above it.

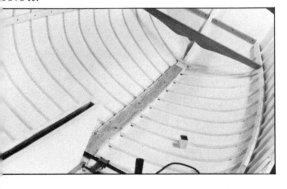

55 (left) The inside work begins by putting in the seat risers, which are of spruce, beaded at both edges. The stern seat stretcher lands against the risers and is screwed to them by an angled screw at each end. The cleat across the inner face of the transom makes a landing for the seat's other end. The floorboards are of 1/2" cedar (the same stuff as the planking) and the center one is screwed directly to the frames.

56 (above) The two thwarts serve to brace the centerboard trunk and are partially supported by it as well. The edges of the thwarts are chamfered underneath, giving them a lighter, less "woody" appearance. Here, the stern seat is shown being fitted into place.

57 The floorboards are more easily fitted before the thwarts are put in permanently. Being fastened to steam-bent cedar cleats, the entire floorboard panel on each side of the boat can be removed later for cleaning or for painting the hull under it.

58 & 59 Cutting the sheer strake and frame tops down to the final sheer line is done with a sabre saw, but first the line itself is marked by means of a fairing batten — positioned so as to be "eye sweet."

It's much easier to get a good sheer line with the boat turned rightside up, and cutting the right angles to this boat's flared-sides results in about the right "crown" to the rail.

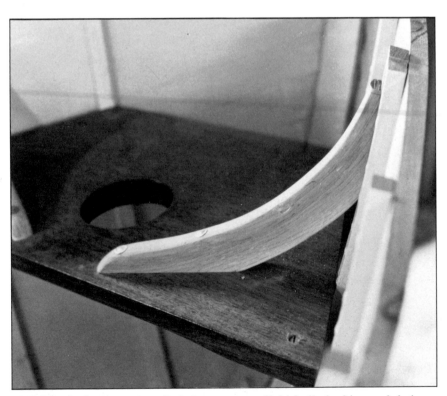

62 Thwart knees are installed about square off the hull planking and their tops are notched to fit under the inwale. A cardboard pattern makes fitting these knees quick work. Copper rivets attach them to the thwarts. The inside of the hull, by now, has been pretty much finish-painted, a task which goes along much faster without interference from seats, inwales, knees, and the like.

63 Making the breasthook of two pieces enables its grain to run along the boat's rail, and saves having to hunt up a natural crook. A threaded bronze rod holds the two halves together with the aid of glue. The breasthook is made up plenty big to allow for fitting later on, and its joining halves are beveled along the center seam for a rough crown.

60 Knees of steam-bent oak will be used in the after quarters and for the thwarts as well. This piece fractured and had to be thrown away, but the others, which were allowed to steam awhile longer, bent around the form

without any problem. A metal backing strap, kept clamped to each end in such a way as to keep the outer fibers from stretching, is a vital part of successful knee bending. Make sure the stock you're using has extra strength for leverage in wrapping it around the form. To allow for some straightning after the clamps are removed, the bending forms are made with a little more curve than is ultimately needed — probably an extra 3/8" on each end will do. By thus overbending the pieces and by allowing their fibers a couple of days on the forms to harden up, the finished, free-standing curve should be about right.

61 Two 5/8" knees like this one can be gotten out of each 1⁵/₈ x 2" bent piece like the one in back of it.

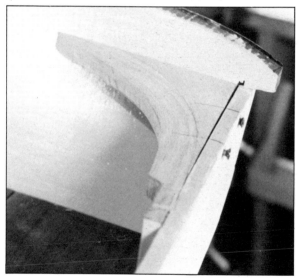

64 This shows how the breasthook is fitted and fastened to the stem and sheer strakes and how the finished crown has been worked into it beforehand. Its after corners have been notched out for the inwales.

65 & 66 With a filler piece glued to each steam-bent quarter knee to fill out its corner, they look just about like natural crook knees and are every bit as strong. If apple or oak crooks are hard to get, you'll probably want to try the same thing.

67 There are a number of good-looking ways to finish off the top of the stem and this is but one of them. A filler piece has been used in the void space on either side of the stem just ahead of the breasthook, although some builders prefer to eliminate these voids by notching the breasthook around the stem. Still others leave the voids open and unfilled. Take your choice.

68 The oarlock blocks are riveted to the inwales and screwed to the sheer strakes. The inwales and guard rails are attached to the boat at the same time and with the same fastenings—a No. 10 copper rivet driven through from the outside at each frame

and knee. The rails are set a bit lower than the sheer strake and frame tops (which are rough-sawn to the final sheer line at this point), so that after installation a belt sander can be used to dress everything down to a common height. A bit of hollow planed into the back side of the guard rails makes them seat well, and if their ends are tapered some at the bow and stern, they look a whole lot better. Of course at the extreme ends, where there is no inwale, fastening is by flat head screws driven into the breasthook forward and the quarter knees aft.

White pine makes a good guard rail, being soft enough not to damage other boats' topsides when laying alongside. And left unpainted, it won't leave smears of rubbed-off color behind, either. Pine rails weather some and turn gray after a few seasons, but bringing them back is simply a matter of taking off a shaving or two. And when worn out, it's no big job to renew them—just grind off the peened over rivets along the inwale and drive them back out. Herreshoff's used beautifully molded sheer-strakes in which the guard rail was an integral part. They're about as handsome a thing as was ever conceived, but are time-consuming to make up without special machinery and aren't easily renewed when worn.

The Centerboard

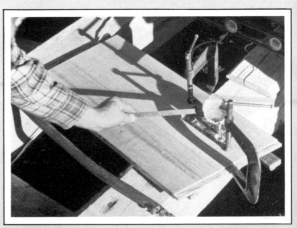

The centerboard, made up from several pieces of 3/4" oak, has grooved caps which fit over each end to keep it from warping, held there by galvanized nails. Bigger nails, about 30d, were used in fastening the board itself together, a plank at a time. Lead ballast, to keep the board from floating, will be poured into the cavity shown here. The nails keep the lead held fast in place.

69 The rudder is made from a single piece of mahogany and may be hung in whatever way suits your fancy. The hardware shown was used because it was available, but there are a number of other ways to do it.

70 Turnbuttons, made up of brass half oval and screwed to the floorboard stringer, hold the outboard sides of the floorboard panels down into place.

71 Brass half oval, riveted to the tiller, makes the connection to the rudderhead. If the top of the rudder is made as shown, the tiller can pivot freely up and down; it can also be removed entirely by swinging it way up so the cross-pin comes free of its notch.

These photos follow the lead-pouring process. A metal plate clamped to the board's underside forms a temporary bottom to the lead cavity. After melting, the lead is ladled out and poured until it stands proud from the board's surface. After cooling, this excess lead can be planed down with a woodworking plane.

Finishing the centerboard consists of nailing on its end pieces, rounding off its corners, boring for the pivot pin and the pendant, and giving it a couple of coats of antifouling bottom paint. The pivot pin is a 5/16" bronze carriage bolt which rides in a brass pipe nipple threaded into the board.

Plank Stock

You will note that white cedar was used to plank this boat and that it is also specified on the drawings. For a small boat, especially one that is carvel planked, cedar can't be beat—it is both lightweight and docile. By all means use it if you can. We feel so strongly about its virtues that we hesitate to specify alternatives, although builders in other parts of the world may come up with a suitable substitute. If you do use another wood, however, we suggest you stay away from dense ones like hard mahogany, which, although taking a nice fancy finish, is a "take charge" kind of planking, which the frames and fastenings of this little boat won't endure. Broken frames and cupped planks may be the result.

72 The finished boat awaits the final fitting of the mast and the step, just before launching. The seat knees in the plans are slightly longer for more bearing on the thwarts.

Maynard Bray

73 Joel White shaves the heel of the mast for a [...] to the step which is just loose enough to all[...] the mast to rotate on its axis. Jon Wilson can hardly wait.

Spars

1—Base your layout on the maximum squared section of the spar so the gage will fit down over it.
2—Saw out a wood pattern to this section and lay out a circle which is tangent to it; this represents the mast's finished diameter.
3—Using a combination square (tri-square), lay off a 45 degree-line which is tangent to the circle. Repeat this on at least one other corner of the pattern.

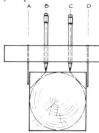

4—Select a scrap piece of softwood as an 8-siding gage and transfer points A,B,C, and D (which resulted from steps 1-3 above) to it. Drill through these points for the two nails and the two pencil stubs needed to complete your gage.
5—Make another gage for the other spar just like this one, sized for its own maximum diameter.

There are only two spars for this boat's sailing rig—a mast and a sprit. They are both 11'6" long and can be stored inside the boat. Native spruce was used because of its low costs, light weight, flexibility, and freedom from big knots. The first step in making these spars is to mark and saw out their outline, resulting in the tapered square-sectioned pieces shown.

(Right) After each of the four sides is planed down to the line, they are marked for 8-siding by a sparmaker's gage.

Sherry Streeter

74 Ready at last, the mast is stepped, with the new cotton sail bent on with a lacing line.

75 She floats! And sails! The light breeze on Center Harbor picked up, and we had a little regatta with Joel's sailing peapod. From the stern are Jon Wilson, Bill Lamprell, Sherry Streeter and Spencer Lincoln.

(Left) An electric plane did the 8-siding on these, but if you don't have such a tool, a drawknife and hand plane will do just as good a job, and with a lot less noise. Once they have been 8-sided, you can work these little spars down to 16-sided, and then to round, pretty much by eye. With the plane set for a fine shaving at the end of the job, there is no need to do any sanding at all, at least not if they are going to be oiled.

(Below) There isn't much hardware on these sticks — a hole at the mast head for a lashing to hold up the head of the sail, a rivet just above the fork in the end of the sprit, and a wooden hound on the mast to keep the snotter from slipping down are about all you need to finish them off.

Maynard Bray